WASTE MANAGEMENT FACILITY

WASTE MANAGEMENT FACILITY

Scott Withiam

MadHat Press
Cheshire, Massachusetts

MadHat Press
MadHat Incorporated
PO Box 422, Cheshire, MA 01225

Copyright © 2025 Scott Withiam
All rights reserved.

The Library of Congress has assigned
this edition a Control Number of
2025937537

ISBN 978-1-952335-98-3 (paperback)

Words by Scott Withiam
Cover image: *Late November* by Craig Stockwell, 2012
Cover design by Diane Sullivan

www.MadHat-Press.com

First Printing
Printed in the United States of America

Dedication

To my partner, Diane Sullivan; and to every member of the extended Sullivan family; and to my great-grandfather, known to me as Drendang, who forbade my mother—whom he helped to raise—any associations with the Irish; and to my mother, who defied him. To all those associations, and to all those who associate.

Special Thanks

Special thanks to the willing and gracious authors who read this book in its finished form; and to early readers and critics of earlier manuscripts or poems; and to the editors and publishers who found and published poems along the way. Also, to those friends, who care not a bit for poetry, but who listen and talk *other things* and freely exchange ideas, opinions, what touches or stirs, an art. Last, to my dedicated writing buddies. I've learned so much from all of you. I'm grateful for your poems, music, books, company, advice, taste, love, and support.

Credit

The book cover art is derived directly from a painting titled Late *November* by artist Craig Stockwell, of Keene, NH. The painting was completed in 2012 and was part of a Groups of 9 Series that Craig began in 2011, which he describes as "A consideration of painting against progress. A recurring look at one thing. Not one thing moving towards completion." Find the painting, series, and more of his work at www.craigstockwell.com.

Table of Contents

                Hymn to Pickles

Draft
Never-Ending March with Box of Tide
Men's Room
Amendment
Him to Pickles
Hard Candy
Figures of Empathy
One-Man Show
Misanthroptic
On Hearing That You Married a Farmer
Where Do You Want Me to Take You?
Bird in a Forest
Separate Cars
Sun Worshipping in Sarasota, FL
Closed Books

                Capped Landfill

Rinse-on-a-Stick
Grace
Space Probes
The Epic
Can Do
Becoming Hat
Future Gifts
The Capped Landfill
Attending Their Friends' Wedding Two Weeks After
    Their Own
Another Pink Azalea
The Best Orgasm I Ever Had

Solutions

Waste Management Facility
The Angry Estate Gardener
Shifts
Tagged Specimens
NyQuil
Solutions
My Best Hire
Before I Let You Go

My Auto Dealership

Poetry Contest
Diagnosis
"We Have Aaron Hernandez's Brain"
Management
Aftermath Posturing
Suspicion
How Could This Happen?
Bob Being a Manhole
No Rooms
Faith
My Auto Dealership
Occupation

Acknowledgments   x
About the Author   x

Hymn to Pickles

Draft

My grandmother's mood—everywhere,
the wind-swirling snow, and racing past the gas station
as an excuse to buy cigarettes just to step out,
escape. The two of us speeding across corn flats
to the lake, to the overlook, where jumping out of the car,
she went sprawling, looked around to see who saw—
nobody—scrambled up—one high heel snapped—
and ran hobbled to the cobblestone wall lining the cliff
edge. There, she hopped up, unbuttoned her full-length
coat, let it flap. Winged, leaned into the storm. Scary,
but I knew she wouldn't jump. I understood she gathered
strength, felt most alive. She called to me, but I didn't go.
I shook, not from freezing, because someday I might
have to do what she did. Eventually, I got out
of her car, stood behind but below her,
shielded and short of her coat's whip.
She kept telling me to step up, look,
look, but I covered my face. The snow, I said,
burned, hurt. Only gaps between fingers allowed
the view of flake-streaked cobalt-blue wallpaper,
the lake with whiter waves breaking. Crashing through,
a flock of geese flew toward us, barely skimming
the cliff, using it for draft. She stretched
both arms up, as if to grab a few goose legs
and be lifted. She implored, "Yes, yes,"
and "more!" to a roused crowd, but suddenly
turned the annoyed conductor. No, not the end
of the symphony. Only a pause between movements.

Scott Withiam

Never-Ending March with Box of Tide

March, drove home.
March, my childhood friend inside

a radiator-hissing, pipe-clanking hospice. My friend
in and out. All bones under a white sheet. March,

as I remembered it, thawing, but snowing outside.
Given, my friend said,

the smell of snow, he'd track, hunt out. March out. But out
of nowhere, he jumped back to opening day, November,

the two of us thirteen, wacky, pumped to drive deer
for the old farts, and then from there, his forward

to another March, my step-father driving
a bottle of Seagram's and two chestnuts into the same

woods. Two chestnuts, their prickly husks, what my friend
and I became over the years, I thought, our lives country

versus city, and all that meant—worlds apart. "Two
chestnuts in one hand, worked one around the other,"

my friend said, "broken out, powder-slippery, working like
ball bearings siliconed to make a wheel roll farther,

Waste Management Facility

though why would you ever want that in never-ending March?" My step-father's car found parked in those woods.

Dead, engine still racing, he'd gone to the head of the parade, was now driving the homecoming queen

with the convertible top down, his friends said. "That camera sitting there," my friend said, "is now yours.

Take it. Take the right pictures." For the rest of that March I drove around with *Right?* shot nothing, while my friend

kept tracking, till that moment, I prefer to think, he left right, when the homecoming queen herself flushed,

slipped out of her sagging trailer to drop off detergent to someone who needed to finish laundry. Thoughtful:

Let me help you finish. The sky just dumped. Wet-lumped snowflakes whipped. *Click.* Overall, my photo's tones

crushed gravel, black and white, except for her box of Tide, its branded orange and yellow bullseye still bleeding through.

Men's Room

When from under the empty highway parking lot's steely-
pink, jittery vapor lights I saw the late-night gas station
attendant leaned back, arched over the cash register,
hands locked behind his head, I thought, *By himself,
unsupervised,* till I fell in with his rapid jiggling
upon the gray metal stool, its round seat rapping
the counter edge enough to split a veneer seam, bruise
the particle board protected beneath. And when he stooped
forward to peek out that gap in an ad-filled window
to see who pulled in, I thought of the unattended animals
I'd seen failing in a failed zoo, catatonic, rubbing the same
spot in chain-link fencing. Same spot on their necks or
haunches—raw. Or gnawed. When he sat back again
and resumed his slouch and stimulation, I almost heard
the sound of board chips landing on a few matchbooks
dropped and left on the floor, the books still stiff, brand
new. When grabbed from the box in the drawer—ajar,
below the register—and then wedged under a limping stool
foot, they steadied, stopped his tendency to chew, to ruin.
They never succeeded long, always worked themselves out
from under. The animals too, but for good. The steadying
match covers, if picked up, would bear the circular stamp
made by the hollow leg where the foot pad had been
attached. When I got out of my car and walked inside,
that wasn't what was in his hand or on his mind.
Anticipating, ahead of me, he nodded to the open door
in back, and said, "Turned on the light."
I meant to say thank you. Instead, said good night.

Amendment

Bigger than my rented Civic,
the Honda Accord, not an agreement,
not an amendment, though clearly
out of my control.

I wasn't driving it—the battered
Silver Accord—as I drove into
a huge, empty highway parking lot
in my Civic. Beyond the Kansas plains,

into Colorado—still the same
plains—under a night sky
full of stars (no matter
where I went, no matter

where I took it), there
it sat, and nothing more
entered into it, the battered
Silver Accord, other than

the late-night gas station
dully reflected upon it,
the attendant seated inside
dully reflecting,

his back molded over
the register, the evening's take.
Him assuming
the only position that offered

gap enough to see
out from under
the ad-plastered windows—
tobacco, power, and buzz

drinks, lotteries—
just to keep it going—
so he could keep
an eye on the Accord

that he worked all night for,
just to keep that going.
All night just to keep it going
would be no name for any Accord,

though now I wondered:
Was that an amendment? Anyways,
out in the great wide open
things sounded better

under those stars or gods
I could identify. It wasn't
a nation's sound system,
just the station's, its straining,

tinny bass buzzing the flimsy
dropped ceiling frames.
This was how he closed.

Him to Pickles

My grandfather laid rail
toward cities he claimed
no interest in.
The day his buddy fell
off their flat car home
and died, my grandfather traveled
as far as his bulkhead, down
to his basement,
to the walled, dank quiet
and never, really, came out
of it, as we say. He lost
one son to lockjaw. He went soft,
opened a haberdashery,
felt and cloth.

An ugly war undressed.
The store failed. His only son
left, but did return and prosper.
As the grandson, I knew none
of the above, only what I loved,
as it should be, him,
and at the base of his stairs,
off to the side, in the dark,
his sweating crock, in it,
bread & butter pickles curing.
The round wooden cover
sliding away sounded
like the cover on a well,
only deeper,
and when not slid back, signaled

Scott Withiam

my grandfather floating up
bright-eyed into the kitchen,
holding up
his pickles in a glass measuring cup,
but not for measuring, only to view
the sugar-coated brine,
swelled mustard seed,
all of those onions translucent,
tamed, then plunked down on the table
between us, so he could say,
"You'll never taste anything
like these again."
More to himself.

Hard Candy

"Always glad to see you,"
she said. It never looked it.
"Got something for your sweet
face." The three clocks ticking
in her parlor chased

each other. One just had to take
the lead. "Don't bite down,"
she said, "savor. It's candy,
Love, not food." Wasn't even
in my mouth yet. Outside,

down the hill, her husband's
mower choked and died
on Tippy's shank bone.
Tippy couldn't be found.
I savored. My cellophane wrapper

swept up—she kept the place
perfect—scrunched—wouldn't fold
in her hand—sounded ablaze.
In the trees, cicadas
taught the clocks to stop

chasing, break out on their own.
Her husband damned the bone,
Tippy, who had hidden it, the long grass,
those bugs, they could all go to …
"Locked?" Locked!" The basement

door, his quickest way back in.
"Time for you to go," she said.
"Straight out the front. And don't run
with that in your mouth"
"I don't have anything …"

"Yes you do." A sliver
spanned the crease
in my tongue. How did she know?
"Finished," she said,
and held out the waste can.

Figures of Empathy

Empathy as the rundown canning factory,
its rolled roof sinking,
its conveyors shooting through
like a compound fracture,
as I saw it. Concentric layers
of fence surrounding the factory.

And the *Keep Out* signs posted
everywhere around it, so no way in,
so no more dwelling, as I did, as a boy,
in concrete block stalls, the abandoned
temporary migrant homes, staring at
their one hot-plate unplugged
and left last minute, worrying
how they managed. Unplugged,
and tomorrow gone. And another day

that factory leveled,
along with it, the marker
to anyone formerly attached.
Not quite. Farther up creek
was the factory dump,
rusted reject cans to kick,
to wade through, to glimpse
a blue cold cream jar
below brows of boot soles,
the glimpse as quick-glancing
migrant eyes averting,
as if staring too long
something bad was sure

to happen, and if not looking
at all, something would.

   *

Empathy running weary
if someone too young to remember
didn't remember that factory
or when it closed, or more, how quickly,
afterwards—the need for canning depleted—

the vegetable fields were scraped,
replaced with tightly planted, waving
wheat. Remembering now, a good thing.
I was not allowed to join the waves.
If I crossed a field, the combine harvester
might not see me or the trail I left.
The alternative was to circle
the field like a hand on a clock
and sample, snap a stalk from the edge,
twist a wheat head to drop wheat berries
into the cup of my palm,
blow away chaff, taste.
Everyone was taught to taste the berries
for unrefined nuttiness.

   *

Empathy, then, that winter the man who owned that dead
factory died, and the wheat fields were unharvested,
and elders said, "It's sad." Not his death so much as its
marking the end of an era I didn't know, just the talk of the

Waste Management Facility

new era I was in but had no idea about, except its promises
of increased freedom and happiness. Still, trying to remember

the migrant stalls, never mind understand how one man's
disappearance meant more than so many others.

*

Empathy, then, the owner's wheat field left standing,
unharvested wheat disposed to snow, stalks bending,
buckling, creating field mice homes,
caves strung with wheat berries to pluck.
Mice flourishing, so much so that my old beagle,
Tex, snow-rolled and snout-plowed,
and never harmed a mouse.

*

Empathy with that same spring
the wheat fields yielded weeds, mostly,
and their undersides were covered
with white spit bug spit, as if the snow
saw what it did and liked what it saw
and really never left.

*

As my era. As an owner.

*

Empathy as that leap to summer's searing heat,
which lingered till attention turned to sawdust,
more the sawdust pile near the former factory

site. Sawdust from the crate mill. Crates to stack,
to deliver more cans than ever before. Every era
as more cans, as the sawdust pile smoldering.
Spontaneous combustion, a fire on site, no one
or any part of the factory lost or moved so much
as moving.

    *

As a pyre.

    *

Empathy not as the factory owner's son offering—
while the fire continued at the mill site—to buy
the fire department a special solution, a foam
which, once sprayed on the burning pile, would seal
the fire forever, but as the homegrown fire chief,
also, once a child in those fields, saying no thanks
to the foam or special suits needed to keep that shit off
of you, because the foam looked more like spit bug spit
and snow, which reminded him of Tex,
and some wild inkling the fire should never go out.

One-Man Show

Taken to but not taken by that one-man art show. Grief.
The gallery's featured artist attracted to roughly the same

landscapes where my recently deceased friend and I grew
up—jaundiced-eyed skies, fallow fields of fall's last weeds

and wildflowers—the wet mix, specifically, goldenrod,
black-eyed Susans, asters, emptied, brittle-gone-quaggy.

Grief. To get past those, brushing by the rest
of the gallery's paintings, mostly thickets into thicker

wooded slopes that on the other side broke to shimmering
lake views, sails, and sun. Thanks,

but to past farmers' clearings, nothing anyone living
had a hand in—no thanks. And not interested in

any artist's abstractions, as in good grief: his "many
attempts to find the spirit, the energy that constantly

animates?" My many attempts destroyed exactly what I
sought: relief. The most visited canvas? An odd piece—

a single flower, once up close live, now crowding a tiny
frame—a crocus called by spring light,

then trapped by spring snow. Left alone, although since
rendered as such, never really.

Scott Withiam

Misanthroptic

Waking. Somewhere in the neighborhood,
a switched-on whir, then the repeated whine of a saw,

till one day pulling on some pants and setting out
to find exact location. Not that far away,

a dead giveaway: BOB BLAIR'S HOME FURNITURE REPAIR.
A folding garage door was raised, rolled back.

Blair emerged otherworldly in his cloud of sawdust,
but wheezing and sucking for air. Over his head,

centerfold pin ups in every garage door panel
were framed by black tape. They hovered like angels.

"Electrical," Blair said, hacking and glancing up.
"No good for anything other than insulation."

I probably looked confused.
He meant the tape—you wrapped it around exposed wires

or twisted connections. Uh-huh. I followed
Blair's curled pine shavings blowing

across the concrete floor—the angel's hair fallen out
the night before. *What worried the angels?*

Above all, Blair sweating about people who didn't take
care of their furniture, so never addressed one thing.

Addressed? "What's wrong with this world?"
Who took care of Blair?

I wanted to know. His hands
ran down the contours of the damaged armoire

dropped off the night before. *Armoire,* I thought.
Something to do with love, right? "Back again,"

Blair said, of that tall piece of furniture,
"for the umpteenth time. The same damn door

broken by the same kid who keeps swinging on it.
What's wrong with people?" I try to forget

asking, "Is this how you spend all day?"
and then, how quickly he showed me his license

plates—uninterrupted years—
nailed edge-to-edge on the back wall. "Memories,"

Blair scoffed. "Memories are for cons, for cons
pressing plates. *Cons?* "They stamp all day

to keep down dreams of getting any time back,
as if next time around would be better."

"Where," I asked, "are they?" I meant memories.
"In prison," Blair said. "Pay attention."

Scott Withiam

On Hearing You Married a Farmer

Those lovely, long fingers traveling
from hanging a bleached wash to gripping,
tugging the bloody hindquarter of a breached
calf. Tugging like mad. The calf didn't make it.
Soon after, you stood outside, in a wild herb garden
below a kitchen window, absently snapping cilantro,
mint. It revived what I loved about you, both of us—
events, outcomes weighed, quite a few odd, unexplainable;
what gave life, well, wonder. And there you are.
It's another day waking to mysteries in acreage,
yesterday's unwashed scents now in separate drops
streaking your bedroom's moisture-filled east window,
running from the small circle rubbed clear with your index
finger. Glass squeaking, a crow flies from trash piled
at the far end of your husband's property. The pile waits
for the new front-end loader to push it into the gully.
Now the crow's erratic flight—hard work flying
headwinds—full-bodied twists with each wing-stroke,
and with each twist, your expectation to catch a glint
in the crow's clutches, a hint of some shiny scrap
from the heap to decorate its nest. There, your delight,
considering the strange gifts I'd bring,
if allowed to visit.

Where Do You Want Me to Take You?

My father's hate of other races hid in descriptions of their being dirty or shifty. Or shiftless for the way *they* lingered in streets, mindless of everyone's need—his, mainly—to drive clean through *their* sections of town without finding another way around. When I was young and in his car, I learned to squirm, part by part twist away, a piece of paper gone ash as soon as he turned, began with the word dirty. And still, some days I think how many times when floating I wasn't with him, and wonder why he'd do that, why he'd drive me away. Did he want to save me from following? I doubt it, though still continue with: Where did his scorn originate? Who hurt him that badly, who turned him? I never got the chance to ask. Once absorbed, where does hate go; how does it move through us? Without a fix, I always come back to cliché, *twist*—everything in his path, anyway, twisted. For instance, the only times he actually said the word hate concerned cats, especially our black cat, Cinder. He named it. He called it with, "I hate that cat. Hate it," and said the *it* by biting down, with a locked contempt no animal ever showed. And here it comes, the only time my mother ever purred, "Well, would you take a look at this." We—my sister, mother, and I—peered out the kitchen window overlooking our backyard, and watched my father wheeling Cinder in his wheelbarrow. He dipped and weaved and Cinder tried like hell to sink claws into steel. How? Why? My father's rare side was exposed. Joy toyed with his heart, and it toyed with ours. He chanted, "Come on, Cinder, where do you want me to take you?" In my mother's hunger for her children to see—or for my father to—she cranked the window wider. He recognized the crank's squeak and glimpsed us squeezed into the window frame, and didn't like that he had been caught outside, so flipped the wheelbarrow, and sent Cinder flying. Then, he righted the wheelbarrow and walked it behind the shed and leaned it there, as if just another concrete home improvement project completed, as if what we'd just seen never happened at all.

Bird in a Forest

The first time my father struck my mother,
I didn't see it happen, but heard a sound
I could only equate with one potato picked
and thrown to a harvested pile of them.
And then I saw the place my mother had been

standing, in the same place another time,
near the kitchen stove, while cooking breakfast
for the whole family, and her housecoat caught
fire, though then, more a *whoosh* in which
those tiny terrycloth loops snapped

like pine needles igniting one to another
at breakneck speed. My father grabbed
the porcelain baking dish soaking in the sink,
and doused the fire, at the same time screaming,
"Your own damn fault. You're not

paying attention!" as in, after the fire
extinguished, the soaked black smudge
on her housecoat was a destroyed forest.
And the trees still sighing hidden
in both parents saying, "*That* could have been

so much worse." Later, I came back
to my mother's new satin pink housecoat,
the rustle of it, as it fell from her
knocked out of it, as hearing then spotting
a bird in that forest as a sign of life

Scott Withiam

returning, not her scrambling back
into the housecoat and off the floor
faster than any flame, but her
as the loose string found and flown
to the living room, feathered,

into the nest of my father's leather
recliner. That's because I had gone to her
there, kept calling, "Mom! Mother?"
but she didn't move, stared silent
for a long time, as if somebody

seated, growing more and more
comfortable before a fire,
though able, finally, to call back,
"I don't want you here, ever."

Separate Cars

Just happens is what I fear most. A couple grown insular,
nasty, picky over the years. I've seen them out there. In
separate cars, they run into each other, so to speak,
at the Costco intersection, wave. No getting right to who
leads or follows home. Doesn't matter anymore. Some
consolation,

I guess. Once home, they must at least unpack together,
put up, so to speak, an overabundance of dry goods
into cupboards, the pantry, and perishables into the fridge—
more than enough to last, though maybe that strikes a need
to bring up that animal incident I saw on my own return

home. They saw it, too. In different cars, right behind me,
at the same light by Steadman Funeral Parlor, waiting
for the green, they witnessed the hawk rifling through ivy
smothering the parlor's brick wall. Unmoved, both—
I watched in my rearview—thought *Winter: the hawk*

drained, desperate, so going for easy prey. A terrified
sparrow burst from the vines. The hawk swooped, was
quickly gaining, till the sparrow's final maneuver. It sailed
through the higher, tight-fingered branches. Unable to fit,
the hawk veered, and, energy sapped, gave up. All for the

couple, later perhaps, to say how much they loved
the whole show. They'd almost forgotten.

Scott Withiam

Sun Worshipping in Sarasota, Florida

May my mother always chase spots of sun,
pushing the chaise-longue—tipped back on its big wheels
dragster-like—across the highly managed lawn,
her gown a released parachute that doesn't slow her speed.
May she always float because the sun's crossed
her unfinished line and didn't return and shouldn't do that
because she's a worshipper. May I always pay attention
to the cerulean blue, grinning Florida U gator sticker
stuck to her slider glass, to project, *I may goofily cheer,
but Warning, slow down. Glass. You don't want to
go through it.* I don't. She's not coming back.
So let this be the day she gives up relentless pursuit
and simply reclines wherever her nitro runs out,
the only mystery being that the mystery she's begun
reading she's already finished twice, and keeps her awake
only minutes. When she's not tired. She sleeps with three
lanes of torrential traffic running in either direction,
while the surrounding stucco walls get power-washed
and the groundskeepers weed-whack around her.
Let her snore to the high whir of clutched plastic strings
that snap and self-replenish, and let her wake only when
the throb and throe totally halt, so she can say,
"Now, where did everyone go?" and then, peer down,
into the St. Augustine grass, and to whatever ant or snake
may be listening, say of the help: "*No worries.* No worries
for them. They've got some racket going all right—battling
tropical undergrowth that never gives up its own fight
for a sunbeam." Never: it makes for lasting streams of
income.

Closed Books

Never had I, after a loved one died,
seen, as I later read, "a coyote lope
carefree across the front lawn
in broad daylight rather than commonly
skulk along a distant hedge
in dusky shadows,"

or, likewise, "hear a woodpecker
tap [my] painted clapboard—instead of
more naturally, tap a rotting tree,
while in search of bugs—to communicate
from the other side,
the departed one's comfort, finally."

All that, too coincidental; solace was too
tidy, convenient; and talk about *bugs*,
complete crap. I tossed the book
across the room, left it. I had to
visit, more, bear my stroke-hollowed mother—
still here, but gone—*at the home.*

Driving there, snow, in sheets,
page after snowy page, swept by,
kept turning till I remembered:
my mother had called squalls *curtains
and giant jellyfishes,* when a child
and living on a high plateau.

She never saw a live jellyfish,
but read up, gobbled facts; hydrostatic

skeletons, habitat, propulsion. I parked.
From the street, I saw her inside,
where she sat, had been wheeled to
then abandoned by the full window.

She had an oversized book an aide
had opened spread across her lap.
Her attention, though, was on the snow
moving behind me, why, I felt sure,
she sprang from her chair,
straightened, pinned her arms

to her sides to deflate her loose
night gown like a jellyfish:
conveyance from her side.
She wasn't done yet,
languidly floated down,
and did her best—I imagined—

now, it was okay to do—to inflate
to conform over the book
snapped shut on both of our floors,
so the real invertebrate could now begin
to break down and devour.

Capped Landfill

Rinse-on-a-Stick

I've been that boy at the beach,
sprinting lickety-split out of the sea,
just as quickly jumping to the tarmac,
shifting one bare foot to the other,

the vendor then handing me
my choice out of his truck,
a gaudy blue, bug-eyed rabbit
ice cream-on-a-stick,

at the same saying,
"Have a nice day," my character
already melting, myself madly
licking to save it, eagerly keep

from dripping, losing to the heat.
That's the game: get as much as I can
in my mouth, not on me. And there it goes—
the truck smoking off, its left rear

sagging from a broken spring,
its cheery jingle distorted
and the orange gumball still on the blink.
I've been that father, who caught up

and paid for his son, but did not relive
everything in him there on,
didn't always watch him in delight
or forget his front covered in melt

or notice he'd become no better at it—
keeping himself clean. I've been that father
in his abandon who, paying, stuck—
from behind Ray Ban aviators—

one sunscreen-dipped bather
guiding her bikini string back
to the strip—landing
undressed-on-a-stick.

I don't miss any of it,
and the good thing is
none of these people are me.
Then why go to the shore?

That boy whining, "I'm all sticky,
how do I get this off?" altogether
missing what distracts his father,
but "Are you stupid?" doesn't miss

for me. That's his father's on-a-dime,
self-accusing swing, although
he takes an edge off with
"There it is—under your nose

where it's always been—
our big, blue Atlantic Ocean.
Just march right back there
and throw yourself back in.

Grace

My friend, Barbara, here on earth has evolved a little farther or faster than most. People are attracted to her like butterflies to pheromone, in her midst flutter, turn jibber jabber, wish too loudly to land as beautifully intact: "If I could kill just one bad habit (on that wish list of bad habits to kill) I'd be a hair closer to being like Barbara, all healthy ones." Ones, full heads of, in your ways, breathe, relax, love. A lot more I experience that oft-noted tuning fork hum in the air trailing Barbara's simplest query, as in, "How are you, sincerely?" I don't know, but followers say the hum means she's graced, a little closer to *there*, the perfection of heaven. Today, we walked along the man-made Cape Cod Canal, which cuts down a much longer trip, which, Ones, I took to mean to reach *there*, you don't have to go all the way around the sound. There with Barbara, the buoy bells *clang-clang, clang-clang*-ing in the mist, I considered her, distantly held in such high esteem, as lonely, though grateful, nonetheless, for the contact received, frenzied as it may be. About to ask if this too was how grace worked, a huge container ship—stacked high with, well, piggy-backed containers—only a guess, really, as to what was inside—slid by. The ship only blinked at the end, and that's when, really, I felt Grace, the gorgeous college obsession who dumped me because there was someone else. There really wasn't. She just wanted to get away.

Space Probes

Around this time last year, the Town Launch was stripped of families squid fishing. Before that, teams teemed, pulled dinners for the week, then left, the way it might have been centuries past. In this one, they straddled five-gallon paint buckets or faded, tilted cooling chests on crippled wheels to hold ice. Some proudly showed off jigs they bought, especially the long, thin elliptical types improved by luminescence, bright, futuristic LED lights evenly embedded along their sides, what attracted them, I thought, more than squid. Without thinking, I commented, "They look like space probes." One teen casting, remarked, "Who?" His buddy was more excited to tell me jigs had pins, not barbs, which wasn't a response to my gaffe or his buddy's testiness, but a lead-up to advice he thought most important to share: no hook to set, so when squid stretched their mouths—"called beaks, like birds," he said, "but they're, how do you say, super? supper? gives? something like that"—right over the jig and gripped, you had to reel your reel real fast, before the squid knew what happened. *Reel real fast. Who?* Two days later, the town shut down *the sprung-like-a-leak- operation*, also called *a collective concern for our newfound stock's depletion*. "Necessary," a resident standing dockside said, a few days later, now that it was safe for everyone, "but there'll be more of them further on." "What?!" I asked. No, he meant more squid farther up the coast. The bitter March wind has begun to ease. Today, I'll test our harbor, push beyond the nested streets, the tight lanes and rows of heritage-protected fisherman homes one block back, in hopes the globes of my shoulders drop from my ears. It's nothing about hearing, only a sign it's warm enough to make straight for the open, then the Launch, and there, remove my gloves, a layer or two. But first, leave my cap on, not as disrespect for warmth or for progress like it once was, but is.

The Epic

On the day my mother told me my Uncle Hank changed his name to Helen, our coastal town became very disappointed by a downgraded hurricane, and everyone ashamed that, all the same, we lost power. Without a TV, there was no tracking the storm, so everyone in town left their home and comfort to witness the wild beach as it really was, mostly a loose skiff, a rare double-ender raised up by walls of powerful waves. *Should it be Aunt Hank or Uncle Helen?* I wondered. And then the chorus—townspeople now walking the beach—began. The first member, like most, wore a rain poncho whipping in the wind. "A double-ender on the loose," he cried. "Anyone know where it was moored?" Then came another chorus member, this one—underdressed for the weather, clearly not from around here—shouted, "If you can't determine if a double-ender is moving backwards or forwards, what does it matter where it came from?" I was the first to reach the skiff when it beached—my mother right behind me—and I got to say what I always wanted to say, if I became what I wanted to be, an explorer: "The ocean settled and I found …" I had not thought of a name for it. It's then I turned to my mother and asked, "Is it Aunt…?" "Look, honey," she said, pointing to one end of the double-ender, "this little dinghy is named *The Epic*." If I'd learned anything in school, it was this: There is no rest in an epic, and if we were in one, such a boat would have silently slipped through mist, and into our midst dropped a hero. "It's Aunt Helen," my mother shouted, before the snapping chorus caught up and drowned us out. And then, they did or didn't? "Should we save her, or leave her till the owner comes back?"
"Let me ask again: does this belong to anyone here?"
"A fresh coat of white paint to her lapstrake planking. No one would want such craft and beauty to slip away."

Can Do

The spit of land where I vacationed curved
out and into the ocean like a cow jaw.
Like a cow jaw kicked up in the woods, most days
I was just bone-white scared of what
was in store for earth and its peoples.
It's a vacation. Relax. I couldn't.
I couldn't even change that.
But in a *can do* way I could exit that loose tooth,
one of the jaw's remaining grinders—my cottage
in a row of cottages on the spit. I beat my fear.
And others, spying from far off with binoculars, saw
that people meandering our beach on the spit
didn't have to be people. They were bugs on a jawbone,
and oops, a wave flipped the bone just like that,
and now people were, specifically, pill bugs topside
and topsy-turvy, disturbed but at least acting,
if that's what it's called. I was with them.
"Aren't oceans always turning up bones?"
came the call from a pill bug that stopped,
and "Yes," was the pill bugs' congregated
response, not exactly reassuring, but then,
in that squinty, mist-heightened ocean light,
they balled up and blew along in protective balls
using the prevailing wind. "Ball up and blow along
with us," they shouted. I couldn't refuse.
Soon I too was blowing and shouting,
"Ball up and blow along!"
And rolling like that, it was hard
to keep straight what any being was saying
or what was going on. Kind of nice,

for the remainder of the week, till the cooling
wind died. Then a lot of fooled people on the beach woke
with sunburns so bad they itched,
which felt like bugs crawling all over them.
And what was I doing, people from all over
wanted to know, that I didn't get burned
or have to keep scratching;
and where could they get the special product I used
for protection? What store?

Scott Withiam

Becoming Hat

For years
in Rockport, I looked to do something new and great,
improve and solidify its bygone seaport
known for its shifting painterly light,
its galleries, its grainy wood lobster shacks,
their backsides arrayed with lobster buoys,
the motif depicted in paintings become
a kind of candied cliché,

a tourist trap. Instead, I arranged
to meet, after forty years,
a lost and weathered friend in Rockport,
in a local breakfast haunt,
a former chandlery,
the only thing close to a candle inside
a backlit neon marker sign saying *Now Serving: Lightly
Powdered Waffles.*

Lightly powdered, for sure,
what it would be like catching up
on two present lives in a town far richer
in the past, but waffled and flickering
was what I did when I saw my friend.
Some small grudge, like always
arriving late—and late again—became tied
to the hat he still wore after forty years.
Its wool worn smooth, almost waxy,
bugged the hell out of me. This was no improvement.
It was nothing great, but small getting smaller.

Waste Management Facility

I became determined not to allow for that
same old hat. No, now I'd do something great
in Rockport with that hat. Ye old Greek sailor's cap
on my friend's head was that of an 18C merchant ship's
captain, and my old self waxed into his chief petty officer.
So there, then, after breakfast, we both lived better
in old Rockport, and together knocked about its back streets
to surround ourselves with nothing

but the best—coopers, cordwainers, and shipwrights—
because soon we'd ship out for a very long time,
maybe forever, and that's what made our hardly souls
look hardest at their surroundings,
and thus, made us Puritans
internally eliciting *This early March sun*
upon our heads for centuries
has been kind, has given all
our winter-dirtied white houses
a unifying shine, and stands no one house taller

or better, except the brick church,
into which all light, thus so absorbed,
disappears. And there we were, in our own ways,
standing before *the* house filled
with the most candles, and ourselves, at least, believing
ourselves sweated of even the simplest old misdeeds,
which would weigh too heavily once at sea,
so that when without a creak
my friend left as my captain, I alone said,
"And there we went, in his becoming hat,

Scott Withiam

to the slippery rocks, and looked back
not at our homes, but on our old selves
long before they tried us,
and saw, in the distance, what French explorers called Cap
Aux Isles, meaning, Point to the little islands,
which people long did,
but were afraid, like candles, to go out.

Future Gifts

Knitters dominated faculty meetings by employing fat aluminum needles the size of circus tent stakes, which (they loved to hammer home) they rubbed like flies do forelegs, when anticipating someone else's meal. Flies, to happen, I knew, rubbed to fly with precision. To fly with precision, they didn't sharpen, they stripped clean. Who cares what anyone happens? Knitters said, while presumptuously knitting future gifts—scarves, socks, mittens—then calmly yielded the floor to hear opposition to eliminations of difficult courses (More than this?). They quickly quashed those presentations as offal, then struck their needles' hilts king-like upon the conference table, as if what next to be served could only be better, which was, aside from confusing, them. Dizzying, but no illusion, they'd spun an increased flood of student rolls at no cost! and kept their jobs by thinning watered down standards till completely lost. Stunned, I could only keep myself suspended between opposing needle points, where the unfinished gifts that hung in the balance were student sails once filling full, now tatters flapping above a rig adrift, far from any shore, slave to every tide. Occasionally, though, a hand slid away from the unprepared, unclothed bodies huddled on deck, to toss those now worthless, finished accessories—us—over the side.

The Capped Landfill

What my dying friend,
too many years not seeing each other come between us,
had said to make sure to see on my drive out of the town
we grew up in: "Do yourself a favor. You can't miss
the biggest thing around." It was dark when I got there,
and in relief, a darker man-made mountain. On top sat
a giant wind turbine, and on top of that the tiny blinking
beacon for whoever might, lacking power
and instrumentation, have to fly that close. Each blink
reached with red reminiscent of darkrooms, a photo
in the bath piece by piece taking form on treated paper
till *Oh, not what I thought.* The only part exposed
at the landfill was a motionless bottom rotor blade—one
huge petal on the full flower wheel blown out of whack—
one feather sticking up on bird's otherwise smoothed back
—till the finest dusting of snow began to show
at a far corner when red blinked on, a picture I'd never see
when young and wandering that region, but hear first—
crystals ticking on a few dry leaves still clinging. Once
heard, then wondering how long lost in silence before then.

Attending Their Friends' Wedding Two Weeks after Their Own

They drank hard at the reception, and floated floor-side without cake, fake, spin, hold, what had proved so trying at their own. After theirs, they had come away feeling politician-like, spread thin, touching who, really, at any depth? Everyone else had been touched, but least of all, them. No longer, though, were they fixed props under a rented tent. At their friends' reception, they rocked, together, cut loose alongside punk-topped Rockhopper penguins at the aquarium, no less, thereafter to be known as their true wedding place, their start freed from ritual trappings. On their way out, there were luminescent jellyfish in backlit glass cylinders embedded in the exterior concrete walls. They propelled upward in gathered bolts of contraction, then floated down, but never allowed themselves to touch bottom. They never did.

Scott Withiam

Another Pink Azalea

Another pink azalea in a black plastic
bucket on the sink countertop in the Men's
Room, swept aside. And there, fumbling
to fuck ourselves still, the two of us.
Never transplanted to a pot, either,
it was long past its season, a few petals
limply hanging over their buds
like shirts slipped over their heads,
but stuck. *Here, let me help you.*
Most of the petals had already dropped
to the tile floor, had been swept
to the intersection of the floor
and wall by foot traffic.
If not crushed, they stood in a grout
gutter like miniature tripod legs.
Let me help myself: outdoor café
tripod table legs. And let's say today
a rogue weather system developed
too fast for warning. A microburst
blew the café's round Plexiglass
tabletops off. They kept rolling.
Look, what happened—darkening
nervous laughter, screams, quips
of "magic" or "powerful"—
happened. Again, not the indicator
of lasting I wanted, but on the way out
this time, so many wait staff prepared
with fresh settings in hand.
After the burst, customers leaving
stepped right over the mess.

Waste Management Facility

So why do waiters hover? I hate when they do that.

Scott Withiam

The Best Orgasm I Ever Had

The National Park brochure found in the park hotel lobby.
It said, "Maybe it was even one of your many ancestors
who, living at the foot of the park volcano, crawled,
themselves shaking during eruptions, to the boiling hot
edge of a receding precipice, and before being swallowed,
believed they stood on the lips of their god
and became one word for that god to speak.
If that was you, what prescient word do you think
your god would have uttered?" Who writes these things?
The brochure missed so much, failed to mention Mercy
Lake, its depth. Or that the still-active mountain cradling it
slept, while hotel guests stayed up all night moaning,
"I came for this?" I suspect that had to do
with the mountain swarming with ghosts. Mine, at least,
flew to me that morning while hiking up, approaching
Mercy Lake nestled in jagged peaks at the top; flew
from that time I dove into whose? eyes at the pinnacle
of the wildest melding ever. "My God,"
said the ghost, who once brought me there,
"we've already stood on this shore, on the thinnest
lips of Mercy Lake hipped to such glory and glowing,
and with a bodiless feeling out of water, so why come
back?" "I don't know," I said, "but standing here,
on this lip, I see us back then as more like animals
living around and in it—rogs, fish, snakes,
big-eyed eaters." "Why would you say that?
I'll never swim here again," the ghost said, then dressed,
but jumped in, sank, not right to any molten end
but to the cold floor of Mercy Lake,
and as a tight-lipped mollusk. No word, just bubbles.

Waste Management Facility

And what did that make me? A greasy dumpster raccoon
feeling around for a clam underwater.
I couldn't even reach bottom, so I couldn't haul it up,
deftly make of it a quick meal,
leave the two half-shells for others to stand in
whenever visiting. That was just the beginning of another
brochure describing a beach at Mercy Lake soon to
be introduced, soon to be shell-less (not a word),
a model for future parks in the system
which everyone might fully enjoy barefooted,
and without knowledge of any generation's
interpretations of nature's attributes. They too,
the brochure said, would be left alone
to simply come as they are.

Shifts

Waste Management Facility

The Works—Public Works—
was the prized summer job that kept us,
three juvenile delinquents, out of trouble.
There never was enough
work. We thought that a pretty good deal,
but it wasn't all right for our two bosses, who,
before we came along, already had *looking busy*
working for them, but now they had to keep us looking
busy too, more work than they could handle. Often,
two hours before a work day ended,
the bosses ran out of ideas for busy work,
gave up and trucked us to the sewer plant,
better known as waste management facility,
because who would ever go there
to catch anyone loafing? And who cared, anyway,
as long as we were out of sight and off the streets,
all five of us? Look, our bosses knew
what they were doing and so did we.
As for feeling bad about being paid to
or about being removed from view
or about cheating taxpayers
or wrestling with the value
of a hard day's work or complicity,
I'm sorry, none of those concerns surfaced.
But the few times I've been asked, *What impact
does a summer like that have on our future?*
I have gone back to the facility
on those days our bosses told us,
"You know what to do!" That was code
meaning the Water Quality Alarm had sounded,

so a fair chance the big boss would be by,
and he wouldn't want to see us standing around
doing nothing. So time for my buddies and me to hustle,
clear the collection tank scaffolding,
where we liked to hang. Time to
plug our noses and take off to get by
the ever-expanding beds of backed-up
overflow, which once dried, we'd cut,
in the days ahead, into squares, then pitch
onto a struggling farmer's flatbed,
who then used our baked good to produce
superior feed corn around the facility,
a break for him which hid us even better.
Our future? Finally, we arrived upwind
and hung out near the pile of rusted re-bar
left behind from the facility's previous expansion,
hung out where the big boss, in the shiny, black SUV
coming our way, couldn't see us—
the corn already too high—but we could see
the cloud of dust rising behind his dramatic entrance,
so confirmation he was to test release
for drinkability—always questionable
whether or not he did, if watched—
which meant pick up a piece of re-bar,
and still good for something, start swinging,
whomp the high grass as if after rats in it,
and holler, "Got one." "There's another.
Get it!" "D'ya get it?" "Nope. Wait,
there it is. There it goes." And keep
chasing. Don't look at each other,

and definitely don't look back.

Scott Withiam

The Angry Estate Gardener

This afternoon, at my deceased friend Brian's memorial, he was sent on—*Set off*, he would say—by a few of his poet friends, but not remembered for his artful poetic leaps, as he had openly wished for. Remembered, instead, for his *real work*, which, according to the first presenting poet, was digging deep, emotionally harvesting, which yielded writing that ultimately moved other souls along. Nice, but that didn't capture Brian. Wouldn't move him—on. More than anything, that poet's speech was about himself, about his work. That moved me to Brian's tale about a brief job he needed to take during a tough stretch, which he titled The Angry Estate Gardener. First day, he and the gardener were on their way to the estate when some fast-driving privileged guy passed then cut them off. The gardener raged, rattled high-speed after a Porsche—in a pickup truck hitched to a trailer full of fertilizer. He pursued, but didn't come close, and the gardener showed up on the job with half a load, which required him to go back for more shit. Speaking of, another poet rose and echoed the *real work* sentiments of the first. That took me to that angry gardener's heavy investment in koi fish. He raised them till payday, when their skin maps, as he liked to say, expanded enough to stock all the pools in the estate's private strolling garden. But payday came on the hottest day of the year. Regardless of heat and stress, the koi would be transported to the estate anyway, from far away, and in junk ice-chests—leaky, poor seals. Brian questioned the wisdom of the timing and leaks. Shut up, the gardener said, I know what I'm doing. The garden fountains sprung nothing but bloated fish. But there, finally, the gardener jumped back, realized, for the first time in his life, that he should have known better all along, Brian thought, that a forced situation was never going to work. Great, in terms of those poets purportedly delivering memorials for a friend, but what about Brian's delivery? His Twin Banana Trees story! After the koi venture failure, the humbled gardener took better stock of himself, safely invested in a climate-controlled greenhouse, then wintered banana trees in it. Come Memorial Day, the banana trees were transported—with better care and timing—to the estate for pay-off, there planted outside the swimming pool's iron gate, so to give off the leafy racket of global share—right?—during the estate owner's July 4th corporate bash. Party underway, the owner approached the gardener and Brian to let them know how impressed he was with the trees, but couldn't get over how shallow their roots were. "Hard to believe they can stand on their own," the owner told the gardener, who now chose to remain reflectively silent. "No one can stand on their own," was all Brian said, covering, all at once, a lot of territory—from gardener to the great idea of global share so far from carried out, to poets—and right there was let go on the spot.

Shifts

Middle-school cafeteria duty, monitoring ungainly, dour
teens resigned to eating lunch—starch, grease, fat—
if you could even call them that, forced down within
seventeen-minute shifts. Cafeteria duty, the trade I accepted
for release from teaching one more algebra class I wasn't
qualified to teach, to kids who needed algebra most, starved
as they were, for equations they could solve in their lives,
at least balance. Cafeteria, which I hoped would swallow
my own failure increasing my students' failure, where
always those two wiry, red-haired twins tormented,
the twins who colleagues claimed they couldn't tell apart,
because they didn't want to face what troubled them too:
failing students, therefore ourselves. The worst twin
had a reddened scar, as if constantly irritated, a squashed X
over his right eye thanks to a bowl smashed upon the home
table by his mother, because the bowl was cracked. She
was on a jag. The worst twin? One afternoon in cafeteria,
while I felt dejected for not reaching kids all morning in
classes, I singled him out as agitator, told him, "Just sit
down right now, and shut up," more for myself, but he sat.
Till I turned and walked away like his father, far enough
away to give him room to stand, be a man, gather steam
enough to land a flying Bruce Lee kick to my troubled
backside, in front of the whole cafeteria. Lesson? Solve
and be sent away. Or lessons? I didn't retaliate, because I
was a bad twin too, though not his equal. I too had scars
and layers. There were times in my past—and in that
school—when I shouldn't have let things slide. He acted.
For the remainder of that year, I got assigned cafeteria with
Artie, an imposing new hire no one wanted to challenge or

set off, a vet recently returned from a very secret conflict.
Artie liked to do watch, as he called it, not duty,
by standing back-to-back, whereupon Artie nervously
talked golf, the wicked slice he couldn't shake, often
mimicking the grip that caused it, so while unable to see his
demonstrated swing, there was non-stop jerking at my
back. Sometimes, it felt like the banished bad twin's jittery
dance, and also, like Artie's dance on the Friday night
dance floor, especially to the B-52's song, "Love Shack."
If Artie stopped, it was when the music stopped,
 so everyone, everyone on the dance floor, could scream,
"Tin Roof Rusted!" It really helped. Till Artie had a leak
in his house. It consumed him. All three of us. Every time
it rained, Artie couldn't locate where water got in,
because he couldn't follow water back, because he couldn't
see how it traveled beams, rafters, pipes, and wires behind
ceilings, behind walls. Every time it rained, a new stain
showed somewhere else in the house. Pretty soon,
the whole house.

Scott Withiam

Primitive

That innocent college couple stepping into the thrift store hand in hand after their walk along the spring-swollen gorge, gushed over the main falls' force and constant thunder. Then mused, what it must have been like this time of year centuries ago, to have been natives, more in touch with seasonal cycles than people of today, and come that primitive spring, a gut sense of purpose, procreation, along with a well-functioning belief system. Didn't they know where they stood? This is the base camp at the bottom of the falls. This is the basement floor thrift store tribe, part of the intellectually delayed (our latest correct label!) workshop. Above the falls is the university stronghold, where, every late spring, students change their looks and faculty change their décor, or either party just moves on to new ideas or visions real or in their heads and push old appliances, furniture, and clothes to the curb, wave goodbye as all floats better for them, we tend to believe. Their toss-off's reach us waiting at the bottom, we who labor here, some of us for ages. I wish I could have told that couple draped all over each other and poking things as they strolled our floor, what a work supervisor, colleague, and buddy of mine whispered, then, in my ear: "It's happened again." News had trickled down from a tributary—the mail assembly line one floor above. Larry had been caught giving himself a hand job on the job again. My buddy thought that the ideal reaction to the going nowhere boredom of accept what someone else doesn't want anymore—what Larry is, and what we are too—that flows downhill. Take it, recycle it—the clearest and most sparkling thing Larry—more than we—can be, and put it

WASTE MANAGEMENT FACILITY

back on display. And Shirley, a country-western devotee who oversees the mail line, had to have, one more time, screamed, "Put that thing away!" Not because she wanted to. That's her mailroom job too—stuff it. At the moment, though, Shirley was probably going through the staff gauntlet for knowing what to do with it. Meanwhile, staff and workers on the thrift store floor awaited our ritual, Larry's return to base camp to rejoin us, our store of stuff we can't get rid of, but where there's plenty of useless space for Larry to walk it off for us, and an inside chance that if that couple was still browsing, still idyll-dreaming, Larry would approach, range too close, as he always does. And did—despite all the time put in trying to train him about safe distance—and said, "I'm having trouble finding what you need. Let me help you." The couple scooted, naturally, but the best part was it would go on Larry's record as showing improvement, because he's badly needed upstairs.

NyQuil

The latest flu strain sweeping the depressed country, what did it want? Misery, what does it want with us? All I wanted was to be completely knocked out for a night and to wake feeling improved. A little too much. I downed a little too much NyQuil, threw open a window, and immediately dropped off. Soon after, Death, or a dead man, at least—flies circling—flew in. "*You,*" the dead man grumbled, "I thought I'd find you here!" and railed about my life as a nursing home attendant, one of four jobs I held in order to float five kids, what he liked about me. But paying for six cell phones and four cars, mortgaging for tuitions yielding what jobs? what future? with costs generally rising like ocean temperatures, and clean water costing more than fuel was what he hated about me, because I took, as in accepted, them all, and felt stronger for it, just because last night on TV the president said we were stronger. "Officials," he continued, "they've got balls, but I'm not sure which is worse, having balls or following them." "I agree," I said. "Oh, I'm sure you do," he said. "Remember how the nursing home director asked you to take my alcohol away, and you followed him? NyQuil was the last thing I had to endure the place. After you took that away, I had no fight left, I …" "I'm sorry," I said, "sounds a lot like me, but I never worked in any nursing home. You're mistaking me for someone else." "Dammit," he said, "I keep doing this. Everyone looks like him." "Who?" I asked. The dead man poured a capful of NyQuil and held it up to the overhead light. "Toast," he said, then tossed it out the window. "That's what the bastard who I mistook you for did to me," he said. "Wow, if I *had* been him, what would you have done to me?" I asked. "Nothing different," he said, "but if you had been him, you would have followed—out the window after it." Suddenly, I felt better, more so, when the dead man leaped out.

Scott Witham

Solutions

Most often he was called by the temp agency to work for a catering company, quite often at fundraisers. That's where the temp was, at a fundraiser, slicing off bloody prime ribs, when he saw the bright knife, at first, just a blunt-tipped, silver-plated butter knife placed upon a nearby fold-out table for sampling of seven cheese wheels. *Cheeses from the Continents we serve*, the sign above the table said. But because the butter knife was the improper utensil—never to be used for slicing but for spreading—not one distinguished guest at the international fundraising event, not one, put his or her mitts on it. Therefore, it touched not one continent of cheese. So, the temp—questioning the actual results of fundraising to move the world forward, and the how, and the who sliced and got slices, and what spread—carefully swaddled the knife in a clean linen napkin and lifted it, not as a butter knife, but a bright and better knife. Untouched, not one fingerprint on it, the better knife beamed in a way it wouldn't in a cheesy world. "So, then what, exactly were you doing with the knife in a pawn shop less than an hour after you the left the fundraiser, if you didn't steal it?" the police sergeant later asked the temp, now held for questioning at the precinct station. "What better place to augment such a bright beginning for the world, given the pawnshop's dim and disarray?" the temp asked. And then, a rookie officer chided, "Ooh, smart guy, *augment, dim, disarray*." And then sell it, right? the sergeant added, then opened his desk drawer, and slowly pulled the knife out. "You're killing me," the temp said. "Look, selling was the last thing on my mind. I wanted just to demand a ridiculous price, so no pawnbroker could ever touch this world. I was making a statement, I guess, but I got carried away." "Right," the sergeant said, "but if that's all, then why'd you run with it when we showed up?" "*You* got carried away," the knife said, "what about me?" "Right there, that's why I ran with it," the temp said. "It made me feel bad for involving it. *Now, I thought, I need to come up with an even better solution.*" "So now we're back to fundraising?" the rookie said. "I just thought better knife, better world, you know?" the temp said. "Not always the case," the sergeant said. "I'll bet you know a lot about that," the knife said. "Hey! I don't care who you are," the rookie growled, "you don't talk to your superiors that way." "It's okay," the sergeant said, "this isn't anything I haven't seen before. Come with me." The sergeant led them into the station kitchen where he poured a cup of burned coffee into a Styrofoam cup, dumped in a load of powdered dairy creamer, and mixed with the knife blade. He chopped and pulled the dry creamer down into the liquid as if mixing cement. "What do you think you're doing?" seemed to bubble up from the slurry, but the mud fixed, and the knife, plunged into the very middle of the cup, stood. The sergeant carefully lifted and placed the cup at the back of the counter with the rest of the sink clutter. "So," the temp said, "the world stands quietly on its own." "We'll see," the sergeant said. "Given what I know about this place, it won't be anytime soon that someone here tries to clean that up, and by the time they do, the knife, so glad to be out again, will be speechless." "Could you really do that?" the temp asked. "Sarge can do anything," the rookie said.

My Best Hire

There have only been two concierges in my hotel since it opened. The first was an eagle, for obvious reasons: overview; satellite-like knowledge of the whole city. Yet even with such vision he didn't reveal everything about his background during his interview. In his past, he had knocked a woman over from behind and flown off with her purse. He did time for it. He kept that segment of his life out of the picture. One early morning, about three years after I hired him, the blue jays surprised him in his sleep, hauled him back in on suspicion. It was mistaken identity, easy to do with eagles. A different eagle had knocked over another woman from behind in the same area, and in the same manner had flown off with her purse. My mistake was that I saw the injustice to my eagle before I saw his betrayal of me, and how that might relate to his concierge job at my hotel—advising people of the best places to go. I bailed him out, put him back to work, secured a good lawyer to set his record straight. The next week he flew off with my best friend's wife, a snowy egret, who, as a favor to my friend, I had hired for her *doesn't miss a move* eye, to improve housekeeping. I lost my best friend. As for losing the eagle concierge, the very next day an unemployed jay applied to fill the vacated position. Right away, I noticed a gap in his employment history. Experience had taught me. "Jay," I said, and pointed to the gap in dates on his resume, "tell me, what happened here?" He had a brief stint at a funeral home, he said, which he thought better to leave out. Truth was, both the mortuary and criminal justice careers were mistakes. They never played to his strengths. Hair did, and the hairdo of the woman prepared for her funeral by the director, well, no bird could have lived in that, or would have wanted to! The jay took it upon himself to do a quick do over, did her hair

Waste Management Facility

into a nest. "Her family," he began, "they went … "Say no more," I said. "Foremost, I'm looking for honesty—from you, and in what you do. You did both. So then, who better to direct hotel guests than you? In fact, you'll make everywhere interesting for visitors, jay. What's good concierge work but putting an emptied nest on any guest's head, then sending them off to return with new and exciting little things breaking out in it?" These days the hotel is full of steadies more than guests. They who go out of their way to stay here—just for their next do, as I like to think, but would never say to anyone else, but you. Discretion, you know, is key in this business.

Before I Let You Go

One year, my class, known as problematic, for being easily distracted and causing disruptions that made us very hard to teach, wasn't assigned a homeroom teacher hired to file and break us. Mr. Lovette—that teacher—lacked bulk and a bulldog face. Our first day, first morning back, attendance began with a trill made by the binding springs of his attendance register run against his open desk drawer, not a harsh slap of that blue book on the desktop. That slightest difference caught our attention, till our circling Roulette eyes locked upon Lovette's index fingers, then, not a word from us, just thoughts like *You monsters* or *You freaks*, words we were accustomed to hearing from teachers, but not in Lovette's case. He, with his index fingers, took our place. They reached two inches past the tip of the middle fingers to their sides, and made each hand—pinky to index—a crescendo. These made me think of ascending gold organ pipes behind the church pulpit, their range of pitches, and where I disappeared every Sunday. I didn't feel empathy, sad to say, for Lovette, but given that our class was more apt to deliver pranks, thought that's what his fingers were, a clever attempt to soften us. Any second, Lovette would remove the fake fingers and turn our usual tactic against us, get poking and grind. That didn't happen. And, with a longer pointer Lovette didn't stoop to pin the attendance register to his desk, didn't vulnerably begin attendance head down like teachers before him, thus inviting trouble for himself or into the room. Lovette stood upright and held us in his eyes, till we realized he actually looked past us, out the high windows to our sagging tenement and factory roofs, the blackened steeples, which we'd turned around to view. "Now," he said, his first word, "when I call your name, forget raising your hand and answering *here* or *present* or whatever you're taught to do before filing out." We turned to face forward again. If what had just happened wasn't disorienting enough, Lovette began using one of those freak fingers to loop name-by-name down the register as he called attendance, but kept looking out the window, not at the page, as if he'd already committed our names to memory. I'm not sure about the others, but somewhere in there, for me, his calling became more like singing, and my church organ bled in to accompany, so that I couldn't really say how many names Lovette called or for how long he'd been calling when he closed the register, preciously, as if he'd just finished a stirring book. It didn't sound huge, but it was. "All present, then," he said. "Everyone. *Everyone* here." That was the loudest, most excited he got. Then, barely audible, he said, "Now, before I let you go to your classes, here's the question: since your ancestors are really you, do you think that you're really where they want to be?" Quite a way to begin a year, but the next day we were told Lovette was not coming back. Another goon, Mr. Terry, had replaced him. "Remain silent and in your seat until your name is called," he snapped, "and when you're called, the simple response, *here*, will do." Post-Lovette, we expected more than *silent* or *here*, and soon enough came the shout from one of us that really made the room go wilder than ever: "What did Lovette do or say that was so threatening it made you get rid of him that quick?" I've never forgotten.

My Auto Dealership

Poetry Contest

I needed to win the Sarasota Poetry Contest before my mother died in Sarasota, so to be flown down to read her a poem written just for her, so for once she'd understand the value of poetry—sometimes to express in words how much someone means to you—but in that case, flying down, expressed in action too, though some of it paid for. So, it never happened. After she died, I won the contest with a poem about winning the contest, no flight included. In the poem, I bought my own ticket. I deplaned in Sarasota and entered the terminal, where someone I'd never seen before had just finished a reading of my winning poem, because it really wasn't me or for the intended audience. And there was a dead poet standing there dressed as a limousine driver responsible for picking me up and transporting me somewhere else, carrying a sign saying *Are you the person I'm supposed to pick up?* That's when my mother called from heaven and said, "It's all right. Who goes to poetry readings there anyways? Nobody! Nobody now, I can join you." "You can't drive, anymore," I said, which I said to her more than anything else when she was alive. Could I ever stop her? Within seconds, she was standing behind me. Literally, she walked right up to that dead poet and said, "Read my sign. It says, 'I'm here to say that poetry can transport anyone great distances.'" She'd changed. "I knew how much you loved me," she said, and let the dead poet safely drive her home. Now I drifted. I didn't write for weeks. I spent all my winnings. I had to find a job. It was tax season. I took a job dressed as the Statue of Liberty. I waved to traffic with one hand extended over my head, where the torch should have been, while with the other hand I kept scooping a circular-shaped arrow sign to suggest that others whizzing by pull into the strip mall, get help filing their claim before it was too late and they fell behind, which my mother never did.

Scott Withiam

Diagnosis

From the dimmed hallway
outside the waiting room, I heard,
"That door is not a toy!"
For sure, I thought,
and to move closer to that
voice, I returned my magazine,

People, to the wall rack.
The blur of one sagging mother
towing three toddlers came through
the etched, opaque glass door,
and out came my ire—
over an undetermined diagnosis—

through her impatience with her oldest:
"Jake!" His outline was fetal against
the glass, and both hands gripped
the door's brass lever handle.
He didn't want to face the doctor,
either. He wouldn't let go. Jake

was my shadow. "Please,"
his mother said, "get off it.
Is that too much to ask?" It was.
Complete occupation. And that glass
door? A toy for making pleas
ridiculous, as in *La la' la la' la la? Peas*

*fall off when a second opinion
cinches it.* "You are too acting

like a baby. Stop being a baby,"
the mother screamed." *Stop being? Be,
I rooted, in my head, a baby, Jake.
Stick. Block. Don't move a hair.*

*Grow long, thick strands
strong as a vine. Bring down
the house, the building of this
freaking institution ...* "There now,
you're fine." Speaking was the mum—
till then—whisp of a receptionist,

who somehow slipped—or grew—
in. Jake had caved, released
his grasp and opened the door
a crack to accept the single stem
she'd drawn from a vase
placed on the side of the shelf

below her sliding window.
That's right, as in *sign in counter!*
She drew from the arrangement
and pronounced it *frees-ya!*
And with that flower in hand,
Jake flew into our full hothouse,

extended it to every seated and quiet
patient. "Why," Jake asked his mother,
"is everyone waiting taking huge whiffs
and smiling like the flower smells good,

when it doesn't smell?" "Because, Jake,"
she said, "*that's* what adults do."

WASTE MANAGEMENT FACILITY

"We Have Aaron Hernandez's Brain"

> Researchers at Boston University said Hernandez's chronic traumatic encephalopathy (CTE), which is caused by repeated head trauma, was the worst case they had ever seen in someone so young. They suggested that the CTE, which results in poor judgement, inhibition of impulses or aggression, anger, paranoia, emotional vitality, and rage behaviors, may explain some of Hernandez's criminal acts and other behavior.

Heard that sentence while out for a walk for relief
from my cramped attic apartment. I neared a huddled group
on college tour. Then, as I passed, their guide said it,
and looked so pleased to have strayed off script, and by
startling, scoring the deepest impression, attracting the
most student prospects; more, perhaps, had attracted their
parents to invest next fall, by going beyond every other
school's hammered guaranty: to locate your child's passion
and offer the best avenues for pursuit. *"We have
Aaron Hernandez's brain."* Not a flinch from the audience
fighting off freezing spring rain on Commonwealth,
in front of the newly donated center where the brain
was held and guarded. Clear of the scene, I marked it
as the thin slice shaved for research, and evident
under microscope the hollowed summation from continual
unnoticed blows like those delivered by the guide. *We do
have Hernandez's brain,* I thought, *and as it continues,
I own it, and its distance from family, friends, life, and love
somewhere asking, Where is your heart?* My own studded
star of Football Nation who fell from grace, committing
and absorbing heinous crimes too. Misguided, but unlike
Hernandez, not brain-related. I couldn't find my heart.
Alive, though, I might what? Return to that huddle
and bark, *This isn't an institution one should attend*

*or a future direction after. In your searches, please
question which college has the heart? And if a parent,
definitely, I'd want my child to apply there?*
If doing so, then guide-like, and just performing
a wild end-zone strut. Do what, then? A toy dog on
the street pranced toward me, leash in its mouth,
master missing. Do? Done? But as that toy passed,
I heard a TV announcer say, *He's broken open.
The ball's already in the air. Wait, here comes the safety
out of nowhere. He's tackled him before completion. Smart.
Better that, than lose the lead. Still a chance for no score.*

Exercise After a Long Flight

If humans receive God-given or genetic gifts at birth, why not just reveal what those are? Full disclosure right from the start rather than the lifetime wander and tire, yielding, maybe, a few small self-discoveries, but never fully manifest, never know how far you got or how close you came to your full potential or design? Wouldn't it be easier on individuals to know? And collectively, maybe, better for a planet burning from unexpected strivers hoarding land, wealth, resources, and now, minds? The counterargument, of course—Then what unknown would drive humans forward?—silly, it seems, and easy to rebut: less time wasted in search; less time spent perfecting, better planet. I'm staying at a Hilton Hampton a day ahead of a Monday business meeting. Why questions like these, now, here? Do I question where I am in my life? Do I have doubts about my choices thus far; about the person I've become or failed to become, my part? Always. Exhausting. To the motel exercise room, then, if for nothing else but to clear my head for Monday's business meeting. If not that, just to get the kinks out. Another long flight. Today, though, I never got to the gym. After my arrival nap, on my way there, I peeked in on an afternoon birthday party held in a rentable side room. Balloons covered the floor. Handmade signs were taped to the far wall: *Happy Birthday, Ames.* Ames: the gray-haired gentleman sitting at a small table centered between and at the ends of two longer tables of guests. Open boxes and presents crowded his table, but the glimpse of adoration on every family member's or friend's face grabbed my attention. Every face, I felt absolutely sure, said *It took this long, but finally, I nailed it, the perfect gift for you.* It occurred to me, then, that one can't directly know or personally realize their God-given or genetic gifts, but others offering gifts to the honored person may, over time, come closest to defining who the receiving person has become. *I hope you're paying attention, Ames*, I thought. *You may never know how far you got, but this is about as close as you'll ever get to knowing who you've become.* I didn't feel like exercising after that, and so returned to the lobby and flopped on a couch. Sunday hotel: dead. I fixed on the unattended main desk, and fell into a kind of stupor, till the desk clerk appeared from behind that one-way window in back. Ames' birthday party over, guests trickled out. The clerk made his appearance to smile and say Come again or to return the checked coats. Ames was now accompanied by his wife, who had her coat on. One of those types, I thought, who values their coat so highly they don't trust checking it. Anyway, Ames and his wife thanked departing birthday guests till everyone was gone, and then, Ames retrieved his coat. His wife helped him slip it on and adjust, then, looking him over, said, "This is the happiest you've looked all day, maybe ever." *Because he knows who he's become*, I thought, and watched Ames and his wife each drag a plastic green garbage bag bulging with Ames' gifts out the all-glass entrance and across the parking lot to their car. Soon after, ready to return to my room and locate a spot for dinner, I stood and stretched. Another hotel guest got off the elevator, headed straight for the desk. There's been a mistake, he said, tossing a coat across the counter. This isn't my coat. It's the same size and make as mine, but look, the name on the nametag. I'm not Ames Wykoff. Maybe not, the clerk said, and covered with, But it's the coat you checked. So, it's on you. *Happiest; maybe ever*, I recalled Ames' wife saying, and thought, Happiest self when known by filling someone else's coat. Wouldn't that be easiest? Anyway, I won't be back, but I slept very well.

Management

I never saw my neighbor, but I could see her patio grill, so I thought of her in her smaller adjoining duplex as pressed like hamburger. And the pervasive perfume of her unit made her bottled propane, its overused valve leaking, begging for early exchange. When that man began knocking, he was starter fluid; and if he stayed, flame-ups from spitting meat. More often, though, during the time they saw each other, he arrived announcing, "I shouldn't. I can't keep doing this. It's wrong." It cooled everything fast. Raw disappointment. It loomed like the milky parking lot lighting—more often dark, because always under repair. Winter, though, was warm. If nothing else, that made it easier to get around. But the change in weather also brought unexpected outsiders to the complex grounds, so unexpected disturbances, and reports of missing items. Property management started to keep a close eye on who came and went. Her man said it was a sign, high time for him to stop. She didn't want him to. They had a heated argument their last time together. It ended in the same way most conversations end with management: "I don't know what you want from me." "I don't know why it's so hard for you to see!" A week later, her grill was stolen. When management blamed it on the increase of outsiders—with an added "you should know," to shuck responsibility, blame her usual visitor on the loss—I heard her say, "Good luck to him if he thought that grill worked. When he opens the lid, he'll find it was already gutted." *Why was that so hard for me to see?* She wanted lasting love, not fucking. I stopped writing about her and knocked.

Scott Witham

Suspicion

Two loud
hard-shell
suitcases—fluorescent pink, fluorescent orange—
traveling,

in between flights,
suspiciously meeting
in the colorless
national park, under what

was left of that row of three-hundred-year-old oaks.
Suspicion—planted by our ancestors. Necessary
instinct for survival, perhaps, but as we grew,
if provoked, it blossomed out of proportion,

estranged, killed, ruined, could be used
against us. How, then, to change it,
make it work for us?
Rows of food trucks

beneath that barely shifting canopy.
In one place, flags,
aromas from around the world,
all in the breeze. Comfort food. Buy,

join, sprawl, discuss, eat. Posted there:
SEE SOMETHING? SAY SOMETHING!
I thought I was. Just like that,
under suspicion, I couldn't be. I mean, I wasn't

anyone. The suitcases were.
They spoke. Side-by-side,
They leaned on their identical, knock-off humans
and chatted, pointed at the models' telescopic arms,

and said, Too long, so collapsing into themselves.
And of the hands' inferior plastic, said,
Brittle, so falling apart on first contact.
So impossible to travel.

So never getting anywhere
warm. Who called it
in? Police cases arrived to investigate.
Other suitcases present at the time saw nothing

unusual. Even though I couldn't be, I was asked
why two bright suitcases would bother to meet
while dragging along outdated humans.
What were they up to?

Since I didn't think I was present, considered, counted
as alive, could I say selling human obsolescence?
I think you better come with me, the case officer said.
How can you take me anywhere, I asked,

if you don't even know who I am? *A good question
to ask*, the officer said, *but in this case, I have no more
compartments to put you away in.*
A fantastic place to begin, I, whatever I was now, said.

Maybe, said the officer, *but any decent suitcase has a place for everything, so what does that say about us?* You may have a problem that needs, perspective, I said.
Try talking to their humans as fitting objects.

Bob Being a Manhole

One hot summer night Judy and Bob met, and within minutes saw in each other's eyes their future together, made fantastic love, collapsed into that completely relaxed post-coital state, dozed off and never woke. They continued together in a dream. In it, they kept waking, each time in an early morning-after stroll in an empty street chock with manholes, the manholes flushing steam all at once. It was hard to see much of anything except what was right in front of their faces. Judy said that she would really like to fall into an opened manhole and Bob didn't hear her desperation, created by his continual need to correct her, as in "Judy, people don't say *opened* manhole. People say an *open* manhole." "What people?" Judy asked. "Where? As they walked through that fog-like steam, right in front of Bob a manhole slowly opened its thick cover like the maw of a whale. "Judy," Bob said, "how about this: a *manhole opening?*" which, at that moment, sounded like a concession, a chance for reconciliation, but by then, Judy had had it with Bob. "Any opening," Judy said. She brushed by Bob and jumped down the manhole. Its cover clanked shut. Below the street, there was drumming, as if pistons of a huge machine at work. There was no steam, though, just hissing. Above it, she clearly heard Bob confiding in, no correcting some stranger on the street—but who? It's then, the manhole spoke: "Think about it, Judy. We have something quite different, quite special going on here." "That's true," Judy said, "but you're a manhole." "Right," the manhole said, "but at least you know exactly what you've jumped into." "All right, Manhole," Judy said, then tell me, what would our world look like were we to spend it together?" "I wouldn't open my mouth again," the manhole said, "and you could escape out a different manhole." But when Judy climbed out farther up the street, there stood Bob. How, she wondered, did he know which manhole to go to every time? There were so many others.

Scott Witham

Mockingbird

Was I sure I made that reservation? Of course,
I did, I said. But I didn't. I was really sure I didn't
want to be indignant anymore, not over
a likely honest oversight,
so fell back onto a slippery end
of the hotel lobby's polished leather couch,
and slid my ass back and spread myself out.

Peering down at me from the side table
sat a red hibiscus in a blue and white
oriental pot. Courtly flower, I thought,
not imperious, but wise. More guests
lined up to check-in where I'd been told—
now them too—"Without any reservation,
no room!" They didn't fall back. They pressed—

"Seriously, do you know who I am?"
"Relax," the desk manager shouted. I did,
and I didn't. I lifted my head to take a keen look
inside that flower. "We're doing all we can
to work something out," the manager said.
So am I, I thought. "Why,"
someone in line shouted back at him,
"do you keep saying that when you know you aren't?"

"I am," said the hibiscus. "I'm working something out."
Was I that tired that I was talking to myself?
I felt pollen on my nose.
"Please," the manager said, "everyone …"
Please, I thought, *is one hummingbird*

Waste Management Facility

hovering, darting back and forth,
one side to the other. "I'm sitting on an egg,"

the hibiscus said—I wasn't talking to myself.
"I'm going to give birth to a mockingbird."
"I'd like to see the manager!"
"You're looking at him!"
I put my ear to the hibiscus:
"My scent used to be jam-packed,"
it said. "I had a lovely repertoire—

hints of lilac, honeysuckle,
even rhododendron. You name it.
And they bred the hell out.
out of me, bred them out."
Bred the hell out sounded
good, given that trying lobby fight
over a room for the night,

but given that, I wanted to know,
"Why birth a mockingbird?
They can be obnoxious."
"I'll never get my scents back,"
the hibiscus said, "but a mockingbird
steals songs of other birds.
And when the moon is right,

sings snippets of them all night.
When I finally have my mockingbird,
and it has gathered snippets and sings,

Scott Withiam

I'll smell how I used to be."
Sir, we found your reservation. Sir?

WASTE MANAGEMENT FACILITY

Faith

Unused red plastic gas containers
with collapsible yellow spouts
brought me back to just the way I was,
a boy calling gas containers cans
because made—not pressed—of soldered tin,

and to just the way I could be—bent
to their deer tick time spent on a shelf
waiting for the brush of one warm hand.
Potentially, then, I asked How, when out of gas,
and, given too many cans, does a person choose

just one can, one? Faith? Today,
someone filling up their tank next to me
had just gone on and on about gas
as America's. I looked inside the station,
at the red plastic rows. No one, he said,

ever runs out anymore—better gauges.
Billy Joel poured out of the overhead speakers
next to those ominous sprinkler heads—
last tested when?—and filled the air:
"I love you just the way you are." More

the way you were—all cans, not containers—
with leaky, flexible metal spouts.
The back of a fingernail run along a row
made persistent bright bangs—not thuds—
till the manager screamed,

Scott Withiam

"Isn't there some other place you need to go?"
I never thought so.

My Auto Dealership

Would be me moved from the Service Waiting Area
and reseated in the showroom, with its bowls of bite-sized
Snickers. Would be me nervously biting back snickers
over the abundance of balloons on the high ceiling as one,
but so much one-ness overwhelming, so much so to be
colorless, blank, so even more to be filled in
as thoughts rose, just to show you where I had gone

after overhearing a domineering, staff-demeaning sales
manager in his motivational team meeting, and then,
watching him—as he passed his open-door—
glare out at the balloons and spout, "How could they ever
run out of white?" Would be me thinking, *Humans*,
when they were just embarrassed red balloons
arranged on the ceiling. And then, imagining a lot

of someone's time and energy going into our strands
cascading down from the ceiling, and how
we're strung together from the bottom.
And then, how that cluster looked like blow-ups
of ganglia. Could be,
also, where my synapses wouldn't snap
to the sales force's just-released-to-the-showroom jive—

instantly owning my own piece of freedom by driving off
who to scream *I'm alive*. The result, to be so defensive,
I knew, wasn't the intended mood, but would be me
going so far as to prepare a balloon statement
for that moment a salesman began to work those of us

moved from the service area to the showroom, and still
sweating the overall damage without significant repairs.

My statement, then, would be roundabout—
to imitate and offset a common sales tactic—
and would describe whatever the salesman's learned
then repeated pitch was, as filling
balloons for his living, which,
slowly letting out air, made us both
sound too close to absurd instruments

on the dash. It would make for a terrible deal,
would be a terrible arrangement for me
to attack my own already attacked by management
for what end, really? Fortunately,
it would never come to that,
only my moving back to the service area
to glimpse, through giant sheet glass,

all the separated blue balloons
attached to cars out in the USED lot.
Given gusts spurred from traffic down the auto mile,
they would take off not one second
before their short strings jerked them back.
Inside, it sounded like muffled punching bags.
Outside, it would be deafening.

Occupation

As a peeper, some clear night, singing for a star,
I'll hear my human doubt again. It will stop
my singing cold. I'll think back to my school buddies,
the four of us drunk, tossing stones into a camp fire,
waiting for one to explode, and talking futures—
teaching, medicine, law. Sparks sent skyward.
Serving our own kind somewhere
became confused with making millions. Stars.
I love you guys, I'll hear myself say again,
but how long are we going to do this? Waiting
for a stone to explode. No explosion. White pine
smoke pancaked and we blindly scattered,
and when my buddies sat down again,
I had not come back, yet. I'd stumbled
to the lake, where, upon arrival, a smallmouth bass
completely laid out on shore to snatch a frog.
I never saw either sitting there. I'd never seen anything
like it—a bass scooching backwards into the water
with a live frog's legs dangling out of its mouth.
Returned to the fire, I told my buddies the bass saw
the life it wanted, and nailed it. Occupation.
Never considered it again. I saw those struggling
legs. "They looked so human," I said. "Sit down;"
"And shut your mouth," my buddies said, "I'll sit,"
I said, "but I'm not going to shut up."

Acknowledgments

With thanks to the editors and staff of the following magazines in which these poems first appeared.

AGNI: "Draft"

Another Chicago Magazine: "Misanthroptic"; Space Probes"; "Waste Management Facility"

Barrow Street: "My Best Hire"

Beloit Poetry Journal: "Attending Their Friends' Wedding Two Weeks after Their Own"

Boston Review: "Can Do"

Chattahoochee Review: "The Epic"; "Management"

Cosmonauts Avenue: "Men's Room"

Diagram: "Amendment"; Figures of Empathy"; "Rinse-on-a-Stick"; "Poetry Contest"; "Faith"

I-70 Review: "The Capped Landfill"

Indiana Review: "Bob Being a Manhole"

Notre Dame Review: "Hard Candy"

On the Seawall: "Solutions"; Before I Let You Go"; "The Angry Estate Gardener"; "We Have Aaron Hernandez's Brain"; "Exercise after a Long Flight"

Plume: "Never Ending March with Box of Tide"; "Separate Cars"; "Sun Worshipping in Sarasota, Florida"; "My Auto Dealership"; "Becoming Hat"; "Another Pink Azalea"; "Occupation

Poet Lore: "Where Do You Want Me to Take You?"

Rattle: "Him to Pickles"; "Bird in a Forest"

Reed: "Mockingbird"

South Carolina Review: "Grace"
Stone Canoe: "One-Man Show"
The Florida Review: "On Hearing That You Married a Farmer"
The Literary Review: "Nyquil"
The Tampa Review: "The Best Orgasm I Ever Had"

About the Author

SCOTT WITHIAM has published two books of poetry, *Doors Out of the Underworld* (MadHat Press) and *Arson & Prophets* (Ashland Poetry Press), and a chapbook, *Desperate Acts & Deliveries* (Two Rivers Review Prize). Withiam grew up in upstate New York and moved to the Boston area in 1977, where he has lived since. He taught public school math and college English and writing, and also counseled for non-profits. He is retired and now resides in Marblehead, MA.

www.ingramcontent.com/pod-product-compliance
Lightning Source LLC
Chambersburg PA
CBHW020336170426
43200CB00006B/405

Praise for *Waste Management Facility*

So artfully staggered, so particular in their annotated moments, the poems in *Waste Management Facility* declare 'it could only have been this way.' Scott Withiam finds surprise in the ordinary and, by finding it, attaches the extra-. His syntax creates a steady live vibration as he assesses the damages found in family and the scrabble of the working life.

—Sven Birkerts, author of *The Miro Worm and the Mysteries of Writing*

Scott Withiam's *Waste Management Facility* is a sustained engagement with reality that produces wonder after surreal wonder, and insight after surprising insight. Experience is here redeemed, not to be wasted nor turned into "candied cliché, / a tourist trap," but to be managed with a facility—and felicity!—that rewards reading after reading. These are poems discovered hiding in the actual world ("No words, just bubbles. / And what did that make me? A greasy dumpster raccoon / feeling around for a clam underwater.") Quirky and quizzical, familiar and strange at once, Withiam's poems raise the kind of questions that refresh and restore the potential for meaning-making. *Waste Management Facility* is the work of a poet at the top of his game.

—Richard Hoffman, author of *People Once Real*

For some poets, the past calls to the present. For Scott Withiam, the past is the present, and it's peopled by those looking after their best interests, striving and stumbling. His compassion is steady and so is his streetwise eye. His poems offer "delight / considering the strange gifts I'd bring, / if allowed to visit." I'd let him in if I were you.

—Ron Slate, author of *Joy Ride*

Scott Withiam is a keen observer of the human condition and what we like to call "reality." But adhering to the dictum in physics where the observer changes what is observed by merely observing it, Withiam nakedly explores the truthfulness behind what he sees. He takes the adage, and the modern emblem, of "seeing-something-then-saying-something" and extends the exhortation, and stands it on its head, by implying that saying something also alters what's being seen. Withiam dives into what he observes, challenges the reader to discern falsity—the unreal—from the real. He demands both outward skepticism and internal contemplation, and in the end sends the reader into the downward (or upward) spiral of the detritus of "seeing-is-believing."

—Gian Lombardo, Director, Quale Press
and Editor-in-Chief, *Solstice Literary Magazine*

Scott Withiam's powerful poems about childhood, family, sexual awakening, friendship, and loss are both intimate and revelatory. But what distinguishes *Waste Management Facility* is the poet's portrayal of working-class employment—the temp jobs, multiple shifts, and abusive bosses that are a fact of life for so many Americans. Read these poems not just for their probing narratives, their often-chilling depictions of all the ways the American dream can crash and burn; read them because they are, simply, so damn good, their language and music rooted in what Whitman called *the permanent flowing*.

—Clare M. Rossini, author of *Lingo*